Who Was Mother Teresa?

by Jim Gigliotti

illustrated by David Groff

Penguin Workshop

For Wendy, who reminds me every day
to do small things with great love—JG

To my brothers and sisters and their wonderful families—DG

PENGUIN WORKSHOP
An Imprint of Penguin Random House LLC, New York

Text copyright © 2015 by Jim Gigliotti.
Illustrations copyright © 2015 by Penguin Random House LLC. All rights reserved.
Published by Penguin Workshop, an imprint of Penguin Random House LLC, New York.
PENGUIN and PENGUIN WORKSHOP are trademarks of Penguin Books Ltd.
WHO HQ & Design is a registered trademark of Penguin Random House LLC.
Printed in the USA.

Visit us online at www.penguinrandomhouse.com.

Library of Congress Control Number: 2015939754

ISBN 9780448482996   22 21 20 19 18 17 16

Contents

Who Was
Mother Teresa?

Mother Teresa stared out the window of the train as it made its way from the crowded city of Calcutta, India, to the mountain resort town of Darjeeling in September 1946.

The Indian countryside was very beautiful. But the train ride took many hours. With lots of twists and turns and zigzags to get up the mountain, the train moved slowly. That was okay, though. It gave Mother Teresa plenty of time to think.

Mother Teresa was traveling from St. Mary's School for girls to her annual retreat in Darjeeling. A retreat is a good place to get away from the noise and distractions of everyday life, and to spend quiet time in prayer and reflection. It was the perfect time to think about God and to get energized for the coming school year.

Mother Teresa was the headmistress at St. Mary's—that is why she was called "Mother." She had taught history and geography for fifteen years. She loved it there, and she loved her students.

However, Mother Teresa had moved to India to help the poor. As the train chugged along, she heard God talking to her. "The message was quite clear," she later said. "I was to leave the convent [a house where nuns live] and help the poor while living among them."

It took almost two years before Mother Teresa got permission from the Catholic Church to leave St. Mary's and live among the poor in Calcutta. She then spent the rest of her life—nearly fifty years—among people in some of the poorest areas of the world, helping the sick and comforting the dying.

She loved the unloved and gave hope to those with no hope. She founded a new order of nuns called the Missionaries of Charity, who have fed—and continue to feed—millions of hungry people in India and around the globe.

But Mother Teresa wasn't thinking about any of that on the train to Darjeeling. She was only thinking of the first step, which she believed came directly from God.

"It was a command," she said. "Something to be done. Something definite. I knew where I had to be."

Chapter 1
Childhood

Mother Teresa was born Agnes Bojaxhiu (boy-a-GEE-you) on August 26, 1910, in the city of Skopje (SKOP-ee-eh), which is now the capital

city of Macedonia, just north of Greece. The day after Agnes was born, she was baptized into the Roman Catholic faith.

Agnes's father and mother were Nikola and
Drana Bojaxhiu, who were Albanian. Agnes had
a sister, Age (AG-ay), who was six years older, and
a brother, Lazar, who was three years older. They
sometimes called Agnes by her middle name,
Gonxha (GONE-ja), which means "flower bud."

Nikola was an important man in Skopje.
He owned part of a construction company that
built the city's first theater, and he was a member

of the town council. He owned property, spoke several languages, and had other businesses, which included buying and selling goods such as leather and sugar.

Nikola traveled a lot for work. Agnes missed him when he was gone, but she was always excited to see what surprises he brought back, and to hear stories about his adventures.

When she was young, Agnes often sat at the dinner table with her family, listening to her father tell stories about his travels. Sometimes, there were other people at the table, too—people Agnes didn't always know and who maybe weren't dressed as well. When Agnes was very young, her mother sometimes told her the visitors were distant cousins, or friends from the neighborhood. Later, when she was old enough to understand, Agnes discovered they were the poorest people in Skopje. They needed a meal, and perhaps a place to spend the night.

When Nikola traveled on business, he always left Drana enough money to take care of anyone who came to her for help. And people often did.

When Drana wasn't cooking or cleaning for her own family, she did it for needy people in town. The Bojaxhius weren't exactly rich, but they never lacked for anything they needed—and they always found a way to help others who were not as fortunate.

Agnes learned early on from her parents to help the needy. She sometimes went out with her mother with food to feed the hungry, and to help the neighbors in other ways.

Skopje was a vibrant and diverse community. As Agnes walked through the streets with her mother, she visited the big bazaar at one end of town with its large selection of clothes and pottery. She met rich and poor people. She met many people from many different backgrounds. As a Catholic, Agnes was Christian, but Skopje was home to Jews and Muslims, too. She learned to respect different religions, and to recognize that all people are children of God.

THE CATHOLIC FAITH

CATHOLICS ARE THE LARGEST BRANCH OF CHRISTIANITY. CHRISTIANS BELIEVE THAT JESUS CHRIST, WHO LIVED TWO THOUSAND YEARS AGO, IS THE SON OF GOD. THEY BELIEVE THAT JESUS DIED TO MAKE UP FOR THE SINS OF ALL HUMANS, AND THAT HE ROSE FROM THE DEAD.

A CHRISTIAN'S SACRED SCRIPTURE IS THE BIBLE. THERE ARE ABOUT 2.18 BILLION CHRISTIANS IN THE WORLD, AND 1.21 BILLION OF THEM ARE CATHOLICS.

THE HEAD OF THE CATHOLIC CHURCH IS THE POPE, WHOM CATHOLICS CONSIDER THE REPRESENTATIVE OF JESUS. THE POPE LIVES IN VATICAN CITY, WHICH IS INSIDE ROME, ITALY.

The house in which Agnes grew up was on the same street as the Church of the Sacred Heart. There, the Bojaxhius attended Mass, the church service celebrated by Catholics. Religion was an important part of Agnes's childhood. Agnes and Age sang in the church choir. The family prayed together every night.

Agnes first attended school at Sacred Heart, and later went to different public schools. Although girls were not always sent to school at that time, Agnes took her studies seriously. She learned the Serbo-Croatian language, which was spoken in that area of the world, in addition to Albanian, which her family spoke at home.

Agnes suffered from both malaria and whooping cough as a youngster. But on the rare occasions that she talked about her childhood, she remembered it fondly. "Mine was a happy family," she said.

Chapter 2
Call to a Spiritual Life

Agnes's happy family life was shattered when her father died. She was just eight years old.

Nikola had gone to Belgrade, Yugoslavia, to attend a political meeting regarding Albania's future. Belgrade was more than 250 miles away.

When Nikola returned to Skopje after several days away, he was very sick. He died the next day. The family never found out what caused Nikola's sudden death. He was only forty-five years old and in good health before leaving for Belgrade. Drana suspected he was poisoned by political enemies, although that was never proved.

The whole town mourned Nikola's death. He was a good and popular man. Drana became very sad. She was too upset to work. The law didn't give Drana any part of her husband's business and properties. Nikola's partners refused to share the land or the business. She was left with only the house in which the family lived.

As the eldest child, Age helped take care of the family as best as she could. But without any income, the family struggled. So in her young life, Agnes experienced both having plenty and having little.

Eventually, Drana recovered from her grief and started an embroidery business. That was not easy in a society in which men ran most businesses. However, soon Drana was able to provide for her family and still help others, too.

Agnes sometimes came home from school to find hungry strangers sharing their meals once again. Drana urged Agnes to "see the face of Jesus" in each of them. She was teaching Agnes to consider strangers as a living form of God on earth.

The family members relied on their faith to get them through this difficult time. They began attending Mass at Sacred Heart almost every day.

Age and Agnes attended festivals and picnics with friends from church.

Agnes developed great respect for authority in her church. When Lazar grumbled about a strict priest at Sacred Heart, Agnes told him he mustn't. She said, "It is your duty to love him and give him respect."

Agnes began helping the priests at Sacred Heart. One of them was Father Jambrenkovic. He showed Agnes a magazine called *Catholic Missions*.

It was filled with exciting stories and adventures of missionaries. Agnes loved the stories about people traveling to faraway places, such as Spain and India, to help people in need.

WHAT IS A MISSIONARY?

A *MISSIONARY* IS SOMEONE FROM A CHURCH OR RELIGIOUS GROUP WHO IS SENT TO ANOTHER PART OF THE WORLD TO SHARE HIS OR HER BELIEFS AND DO CHARITABLE WORK. THEY OFTEN PREACH, TEACH IN SCHOOLS, AND HELP THE COMMUNITY IN OTHER WAYS, SUCH AS BUILDING HOMES AND DIGGING WELLS. BY DOING SO, MISSIONARIES HOPE TO CONVERT OTHERS TO THEIR RELIGION AND SPREAD THEIR FAITH.

Every year, Agnes and her family went to the shrine of the Lady of Letnice with other people from their church. They believed the mountainous area of Montenegro was good for Agnes's physical health. They also believed it was good for their spiritual health. Agnes felt that when she was there, God was calling her to a spiritual life.

She was certain he was asking her to serve others. When she was twelve years old, she told her mother about it. Drana thought Agnes was too young to make such a life-changing decision.

Agnes was always very persistent, though. When she put her mind to something, she didn't give up. By the time she was fourteen, Agnes was teaching Sunday school to children at church.

Agnes also joined a group called the Sodality of the Blessed Virgin Mary—a Catholic society for young people to honor the mother of Jesus, to pray, and to serve the poor.

When Agnes was eighteen, she told Drana she was still interested in becoming a missionary nun. "By then, I realized my vocation was towards the poor," she said. But she didn't feel it was her decision. "It was the will of God," she said. "He made the choice."

Chapter 3
Leaving Home

Drana still wasn't convinced Agnes was ready to become a nun. Also, if Agnes became a missionary, Drana might never see her daughter again. When eighteen-year-old Agnes told her mother that she still wanted to be a nun, Drana shut herself in her room and prayed for a whole day, straight through!

After twenty-four hours, Drana emerged to give Agnes her support. Drana knew her daughter had to follow her heart.

Lazar wasn't as understanding, though. Agnes's brother had left home in 1924 to attend military school. By 1928, he was an officer in the Albanian military. He was upset because he felt that Agnes was giving up everything— all material things, that is.

LAZAR

He wrote to his younger sister, asking her if she realized what she was doing. Agnes wrote back: "Lazar, you say that you are important because you are an officer serving the king of two million people. But I am serving the King of the whole world!"

Father Jambrenkovic knew that the Sisters of the Institute of the Blessed Virgin Mary—

more commonly called the Loreto Order—had worked in India for a long time. They were eager to bring Christianity to the largely Hindu and Muslim population. They also wanted to help the many needy people there. The Loreto Order had arrived in India in 1841 to open a school in Calcutta. Agnes applied to the Loreto Order and was accepted.

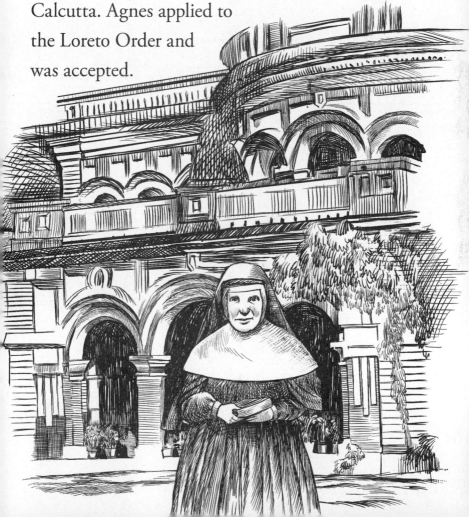

Late in September 1928, Agnes's friends came to the Bojaxhiu house for a farewell party. The next day, many of them were also at the train station, waving good-bye as Agnes, Age, and Drana left Skopje for Zagreb, Yugoslavia.

In Zagreb, Agnes parted ways with her sister and her mother in a tearful good-bye. Drana had feared she would never see Agnes again— and she was right. This was the last time Agnes ever saw her mother or her sister.

Agnes met another young woman who was joining the Loreto Order. Her name was Betike Kanjc. Together, Agnes and Betike took the train to France. There, they would meet with the Mother Superior—the nun in charge—at the Loreto Order house in Paris. The Mother Superior wanted to be sure they were ready for the religious life. Neither Agnes nor Betike spoke French, but an interpreter helped them out.

Agnes was anxious to get to India to begin helping the poor. But there was work to do before that. She didn't speak English, which she would need to know to work in India. This was during the time of the British Raj, when India was under the direct rule of the British government.

(*Raj* means *rule* in Hindi.) The British Raj began in 1858 and lasted nearly one hundred years. So Agnes and Betike were soon back on the road, this time by train and boat, to Dublin, Ireland.

In Dublin, Agnes and Betike stayed at the Loreto Order's main house. It was a huge convent housed in a redbrick-and-gray-stone mansion that was built in 1725. They spent six weeks there learning English and studying to become nuns.

Agnes and Betike weren't even allowed
to speak to each other in anything *but*
English. They had to learn their new
language quickly.

Dublin, Ireland

Italy

By the end of November 1928, Agnes and
Betike finally were ready to go to India. They
took a train from Ireland to Italy, where they
boarded the boat that would take them to
Bombay, India, the city now called Mumbai.

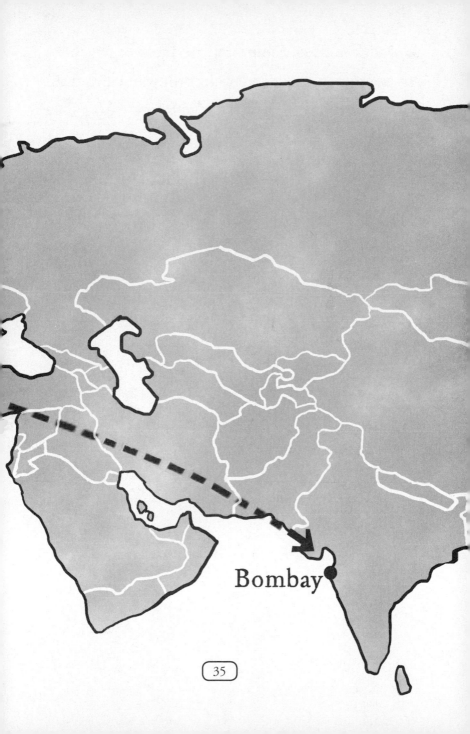

Bombay

On the boat, Agnes and Betike met several nuns from another order, and they all celebrated Christmas together. Soon it was New Year's Day 1929, and Agnes was getting closer to starting her new life in India.

Chapter 4
To India

Early in January 1929, Agnes arrived in India, in the city of Madras (now called Chennai). The port city of Madras had so many different colors, sights, and smells that Agnes had never experienced before!

But it also had many poor people who made Agnes's heart ache. She saw one family gathered around a relative who had died in the street . . . other families who slept outside on mats made from palm leaves . . . still others who didn't even have that, but simply slept on the bare ground. Agnes sailed up the Indian coast to Calcutta (now called Kolkata), for the first time on January 6, 1929.

After ten days in Calcutta, Agnes took her first train ride to Darjeeling. The town of Darjeeling is famous around the world for growing the tea of the same name. It is located high above sea level—the average elevation is more than one mile—so the weather is much cooler than in many other parts of India. It has many beautiful plants, flowers, and animals. But Agnes wasn't there for the scenery.

She was in Darjeeling to continue preparing to become a nun.

At the Loreto Convent in Darjeeling, Agnes studied English, Bengali, and Hindi for two years, while also teaching children at the convent school.

LORETO CONVENT

While Hindi was the official language of India, Bengali was spoken in Calcutta. Her father's ability to speak many languages must have rubbed off on Agnes, because she learned them all quickly.

She spoke excellent English—though with a heavy European accent—and also talked easily with many people in India.

On May 24, 1931, Agnes took her first vows as a nun. Now she became Sister Teresa. She took the name Teresa after a French saint who was only twenty-four when she died in 1897.

Sister Teresa (Agnes) had much in common with Saint Thérèse. She had been called "flower bud," and Saint Thérèse was known as "the Little Flower." They were both known for their simplicity and practicality. And Saint Thérèse, who had been a nun, was a patron saint of missionaries—an inspiration to Sister Teresa.

Agnes spelled her name the Spanish way, *Teresa*, because

SAINT THÉRÈSE OF LISIEUX

there already was a Sister Marie-Thérèse at Loreto. The schoolchildren started calling Sister Teresa "Bengali Teresa" since she spoke their language so well.

Not long after taking her vows, Sister Teresa went back to Calcutta. She began teaching the girls at St. Mary's. The school was located within

the high white walls that separated the Loreto
Convent from the bustling city outside.

For much of the next seventeen years, Sister
Teresa's daily routine was the same. She was up
at five thirty in the morning for some quiet time
before Mass at 6:00 a.m. Then came prayer time,
breakfast, and school. After school, there was office
work, afternoon tea, and correcting papers. Then
dinner, evening prayers, and bedtime.

RELIGIOUS VOWS

A ROMAN CATHOLIC NUN PUBLICLY "VOWS"—OR PLEDGES—HER COMMITMENT TO THE CHURCH. SHE PROMISES TO OBSERVE POVERTY, CHASTITY, AND OBEDIENCE AS PART OF HER CALLING TO SERVE GOD.

THE VOW OF POVERTY MEANS THE NUN WILL NOT OWN THINGS. SHE WILL LIVE IN A COMMUNITY OF OTHER NUNS AND SHARE FOOD AND POSSESSIONS. THE VOW OF CHASTITY MEANS SHE WILL NOT ENTER A ROMANTIC RELATIONSHIP AND WILL NEVER MARRY. THE VOW OF OBEDIENCE MEANS SHE WILL OBEY HER LEADERS IN THE CHURCH.

AFTER HER VOWS, A NUN WEARS A RING ON HER RIGHT RING FINGER TO SYMBOLIZE THAT SHE IS "MARRIED" TO THE CHURCH. IN SOME ORDERS, LIKE MOTHER TERESA'S LORETO ORDER, THE VOWS ARE TAKEN AGAIN AFTER SEVERAL YEARS, AND ARE CONSIDERED "FINAL VOWS." SISTER TERESA TOOK HER FINAL VOWS IN 1937.

In 1944, the Mother Superior at St. Mary's became ill. Sister Teresa was hardworking and organized, and she knew how the school functioned, due to her long service there. So she took over the Mother Superior's duties, and she would be known as Mother Teresa the rest of her life.

Mother Teresa found comfort in the discipline of her routine, and joy in teaching the students. "I loved teaching," Mother Teresa said, "and in Loreto, I was the happiest nun in the world."

Chapter 5
A Long Wait

Mother Teresa wrote to her mother about how happy teaching made her. Drana was glad to hear that. However, she also reminded her daughter that she went to India to help the poor.

That was not so easy at Loreto. Mother Teresa was a cloistered nun. She had to live and work within the convent. Rarely was she allowed outside.

Still, Mother Teresa knew what was going on outside the convent walls. She could see into the slums from her bedroom window.

With 1.2 million people, Calcutta was already the third-largest city in India when Mother Teresa arrived. It was hot and crowded. It had many poor neighborhoods, called *slums*, including Motijhil.

The poorest people lived in the worst conditions
in Motijhil, just outside the convent walls.

In 1943, the Bengal famine sent thousands of people from the countryside into the city of Calcutta in search of food. Conditions in the slums grew even worse.

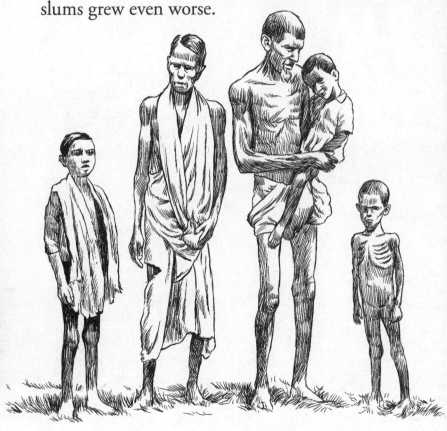

At the time, political leaders such as Mahatma Gandhi were encouraging India to gain independence from British rule. Both Hindus and Muslims agreed on independence. But they fought each other for political power, even as Gandhi preached nonviolence.

Mother Teresa prayed for the poor in Calcutta. Even so, she always believed action should accompany prayer. So she organized a local chapter of the Sodality of the Blessed Virgin Mary at St. Mary's. The schoolgirls who joined went into the city once a week, delivering food and medicine to the poor, or visiting the local hospital.

In August 1946, fighting between Hindus and Muslims grew into a bloody battle that lasted for days in the streets of Calcutta. At least five thousand people were killed. Many more were injured.

Food delivery was impossible, and soon the Loreto Convent had nothing to feed the more than two hundred girls there. Mother Teresa had no choice but to go outside the convent looking for food. She witnessed a terrible scene: injured people and dead bodies left in the streets. Fortunately, some British soldiers saw Mother Teresa wandering in search of food. They rushed her into their truck, found enough rice to last the girls for several days, and brought Mother Teresa back to the convent.

It was an upsetting experience. It must have still been on Mother Teresa's mind when she left on the train for Darjeeling several weeks later for her annual retreat. That's when she received her message from God to go into the slums and work with and live among the poor.

That wasn't a simple matter, though. Because she was cloistered, Mother Teresa needed permission from the head of the Catholic Church—Pope Pius XII in Rome. And she needed the archbishop of Calcutta to make the request for her. Without their approval, Mother Teresa would be breaking her vow of obedience. Her respect for the church wouldn't allow her to do that.

POPE PIUS XII

So, after returning from her retreat, she asked
Father Celeste Van Exem, a local priest, for help.

Father Van Exem told the archbishop
what Mother Teresa hoped to do. At first, the
archbishop didn't want Mother Teresa to go to
the slums. He thought it was unsafe and unwise.

So he told Mother Teresa to wait one year and see if she'd change her mind. But Mother Teresa was as persistent as ever. When the year was up, she still wanted to serve the poor in the slums where they lived.

The archbishop warned Mother Teresa that Pope Pius might ask her to leave her religious order to work in the slums. Mother Teresa had been a nun all her adult life. But she felt she had to take that chance. Months passed. Mother Teresa prayed. And she waited.

Nearly two years after Father Van Exem first met with the archbishop, the pope agreed to let Mother Teresa remain a nun and live outside the convent walls.

There was a catch, though. She could move ahead with her plan only on a one-year trial basis. Then they would decide if she could continue. Mother Teresa readily agreed.

MAHATMA GANDHI (1869–1948)

MAHATMA GANDHI, BORN MOHANDAS KARAMCHAND GANDHI, WAS THE LEADER OF INDIA'S INDEPENDENCE MOVEMENT. HE IS KNOWN FOR PROMOTING NONVIOLENT MEANS TO END OPPRESSION.

GANDHI WAS A HINDU WHO STUDIED LAW IN ENGLAND. FOR TWENTY YEARS HE LIVED IN SOUTH AFRICA, WORKING TO END ANTI-INDIAN DISCRIMINATION. IN 1914, HE RETURNED TO HIS HOMELAND. THERE, HE BEGAN A CAMPAIGN OF PEACEFUL DISOBEDIENCE TO END BRITISH RULE.

GANDHI'S PHILOSOPHY OF LIFE WAS CALLED *SATYAGRAHA*—OR "TRUTH FORCE." *SATYAGRAHA* WAS BASED ON THE THREE PRINCIPLES OF NONCOOPERATION, NONVIOLENCE, AND NONPOSSESSION.

Chapter 6
Into the Slums

Ever since her vows,
Mother Teresa had worn
the black-and-white
habit (the working
clothes) of a nun. But
that wouldn't do in the
city streets. She wanted
to be one of the people,
not stand apart from
them. So she chose to wear
a sari. The traditional dress
of Indian women, the sari
is made from one piece of
cloth that is wrapped
and draped over the body.

A sari can be plain, or decorated with patterns and embroidery. Mother Teresa chose a simple white sari with blue stripes (because Catholics associate blue with Mary, the mother of Jesus).

On August 17, 1948, Mother Teresa walked out of the Loreto Convent and into the slums of Motijhil. She called leaving St. Mary's School the most difficult thing she had ever done, "an even harder sacrifice for me than leaving my family." She had hardly any money on her: only three rupees—about two and a half cents! She had only a bit of medical training. At the convent, she always knew she had a bed in which to sleep, food to eat, and a place to work. Now, she didn't know where she would sleep or what she would eat or how she would work.

She found a place to sleep by knocking on the door of the Little Sisters of the Poor. This was a Roman Catholic organization that helps the elderly. Mother Teresa asked to use one of the empty beds. She also got a little bit of money from a local priest.

As for work, she didn't even know where to begin. So she started with what she knew: teaching. Under a tree not far from the convent walls, Mother Teresa grabbed a stick.

By drawing in the dirt, she began teaching a couple of children the Bengali alphabet. Each week, more children gathered—by the end of the first month, more than twenty of them came each day!

Word soon spread, and the families in the slums were delighted. They didn't have much money. However, they helped out in whatever way they could. One person donated a chair on which Mother Teresa could sit. Others brought slates and chalk, a table, and a few more chairs. Mother Teresa didn't have a building, but she had a school.

Mother Teresa began passing out bars of soap as a reward for attending classes and learning lessons. Staying clean was an important way for children in the slums to keep from getting sick.

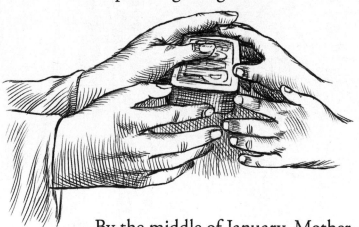

By the middle of January, Mother Teresa had forty-six children in her little school.

She rented two rooms with the money she still had left from the parish priest.

Mother Teresa quickly became known in the neighborhood. But she wanted to be even more a part of it. Her room at the Little Sisters of the Poor was not in Motijhil. She wanted to be closer to the people she worked with every day.

With Father Van Exem's help, Mother Teresa asked a local man named Alfred Gomes if she could rent a spare room in his family's home. Gomes let her stay for free. He even offered to decorate the room. But Mother Teresa wanted only a bed and a table at which to write.

A year went by. The archbishop gave Mother Teresa permission to continue her mission. One day in March 1949, one of Mother Teresa's former students at St. Mary's knocked on her bedroom door. She wanted to help serve the poor, too. Then another came. And another. And another.

The young women had been inspired by Mother Teresa's work in Motijhil. By the end of 1949, there were ten such graduates of St. Mary's. Alfred Gomes had to build a new room and a bathroom to fit them all into the house!

Mother Teresa applied to Rome to form a new order of nuns called the Missionaries of Charity. Her request was approved in 1950.

SPINNING MOVEMENT

MOTHER TERESA'S CHOICE TO WEAR A SARI WAS A PRACTICAL ONE. IT WAS SIMPLE, EASY TO WEAR, AND KEPT HER WARM IN WINTER AND COOL IN SUMMER. FOR MANY INDIAN WOMEN, THOUGH, A SARI IS A SYMBOL OF ECONOMIC INDEPENDENCE.

MAHATMA GANDHI BEGAN THE SPINNING MOVEMENT IN INDIA IN THE 1920S. HE URGED INDIAN WOMEN TO SPIN THEIR OWN THREAD AND YARN FROM RAW COTTON ON A SPINNING WHEEL.

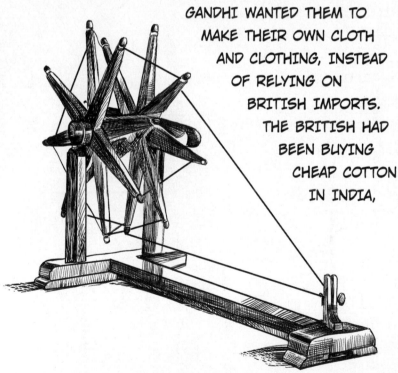

GANDHI WANTED THEM TO MAKE THEIR OWN CLOTH AND CLOTHING, INSTEAD OF RELYING ON BRITISH IMPORTS. THE BRITISH HAD BEEN BUYING CHEAP COTTON IN INDIA,

MAKING CLOTHES IN BRITAIN, AND THEN SELLING THEM AT HIGH PRICES TO THE INDIAN PEOPLE. BY SPINNING THEIR OWN COTTON INTO CLOTH, INDIANS BECAME LESS RELIANT ON THE BRITISH.

THE MOVEMENT WAS SO IMPORTANT TO INDIA THAT A SPINNING WHEEL WAS DEPICTED ON THE COUNTRY'S ORIGINAL FLAG. TO THIS DAY, ONLY HAND-SPUN CLOTH IS ALLOWED IN THE OFFICIAL MANUFACTURE OF THE INDIAN FLAG.

Chapter 7
Poorest of the Poor

Mother Teresa's Missionaries of Charity took the usual vows of poverty, chastity, and obedience. But they added another vow: to serve the "poorest of the poor." Each day, they got up at four thirty, said prayers, had breakfast, then went into the slums of Calcutta. In the slums, housing was overcrowded and falling apart. There was little fresh air. Basic services such as clean water, electricity, and garbage pickup didn't exist. Diseases spread quickly in these conditions.

One day, in 1952, Mother Teresa saw a woman lying in the street. Rats had eaten away part of her flesh. Her wounds were crawling with maggots. No one stopped to help her. So Mother Teresa, herself a small person, picked up the dying woman and took her to the hospital. The hospital refused to help.

The woman's life could not be saved, a nurse said. Neither the woman nor Mother Teresa had any money to pay the hospital.

Mother Teresa wouldn't take no for an answer. The nurse gave in. Mother Teresa knew the woman would not survive. But she also knew that the woman didn't deserve to die in the street like an animal. Caring for the dying was a supreme act of love for Mother Teresa.

Mother Teresa knew from walking the streets of Motijhil that there were many more people just like that woman. The population of cities was growing at such a fast pace. There was not enough room for everyone. People who used to do farm work moved to the city looking for work. They had no family or friends there. Mother Teresa felt that all these "poorest of the poor" deserved her help.

So she went to the city officials to ask for a place to establish a home for the dying. Again, Mother Teresa wouldn't take no for an answer.

They gave her an abandoned building behind a
large Hindu temple.

Mother Teresa and the Missionaries of Charity
scrubbed the floors and cleaned the walls and
brought in beds. In just one week, the home for
the dying opened. It was called Nirmal Hriday,
which means "the Place of the Pure Heart."

The Nirmal Hriday building had once been used by travelers visiting the temple. This caused controversy. Hindus feared Mother Teresa would try to convert her dying patients to Christianity. But Mother Teresa made sure that each patient received the holy rituals they desired. That included water from the Ganges river (considered holy) on the lips for Hindus, and readings from the Koran (sacred scripture) for Muslims. When her Hindu neighbors saw this, they welcomed the home for the dying. In fact, many offered their help.

Mother Teresa provided love and care for not only people at the end of their lives, but for those at the beginning, as well.

Sometimes babies of the poor were left abandoned in police stations or at hospitals or on street corners. The Missionaries of Charity took them in. Mother Teresa spread the word that all children would receive care. In 1955, she opened a home for orphans and abandoned babies.

At the time, leprosy was a serious and widespread skin disease in India. Leprosy was caused by an infection, which spread quickly in the poor living conditions in the slums. It was very disfiguring. People could lose fingers, toes, or features on their faces. It also caused terrible nerve damage and muscle weakness. Lepers were treated as outcasts. No one healthy wanted to go near them.

Mother Teresa opened a clinic for lepers in Calcutta, and bought a van to act as a mobile treatment center. Then she helped build a village for lepers. Now they had a place where they could learn to live on their own. It was called Shanti Nagar, which means "City of Peace."

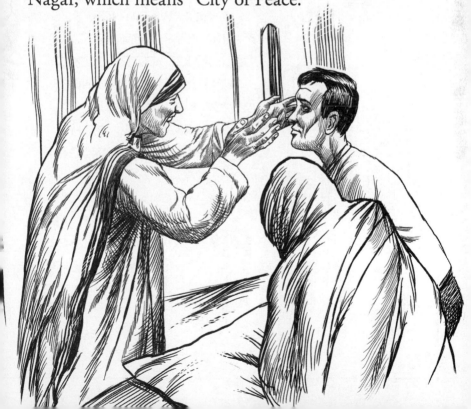

THE CASTE SYSTEM IN INDIA

IN TRADITIONAL INDIAN CULTURE, PEOPLE WERE DIVIDED INTO DIFFERENT SOCIAL LEVELS, OR CASTES.

PRIESTS AND TEACHERS MADE UP THE HIGHEST CASTE, CALLED BRAHMAN. NEXT CAME KSHATRIYAS, THE WARRIORS AND ROYALTY. THE VAISHYA CASTE INCLUDED LANDOWNERS, MERCHANTS, AND FARMERS. THE SUDRAS MADE UP THE LOWEST CASTE; THESE WERE WORKERS AND CRAFTSMEN. PEOPLE COULD NOT MARRY OUTSIDE THEIR CASTE. THEY WERE NOT EVEN ALLOWED TO SHARE A MEAL WITH THOSE FROM ANOTHER CASTE!

ONE GROUP OF PEOPLE WERE CONSIDERED SO LOW, THEY WERE OUTSIDE THE CASTE SYSTEM.

THEY WERE CALLED *UNTOUCHABLES*. MANY OF THEM LIVED IN THE SLUMS. UNTOUCHABLES HAD THE DIRTIEST JOBS, SUCH AS SWEEPING STREETS AND HANDLING GARBAGE. IN 1950, UNTOUCHABLES WERE GIVEN EQUAL RIGHTS UNDER THE LAW, BUT MANY STILL FACE PREJUDICE TODAY.

Chapter 8
Missionaries of Charity Goes Global

By early 1953, Mother Teresa's order was outgrowing the Gomeses' home. The archbishop helped her buy a building in Calcutta. Today, it still serves as the headquarters for the Missionaries of Charity.

Despite such rapid growth, the Missionaries of

Charity was still largely unknown outside of India. That was okay with Mother Teresa. She never needed publicity. She certainly didn't go seeking it—not even for the sake of raising money.

Money and supplies were always needed. But Mother Teresa was a firm believer that God would provide—and she was never afraid to ask on God's behalf!

For instance, when Mother Teresa first started out in the slums of Calcutta, sick people began asking for medicine. Mother Teresa had neither medicine nor the money to buy it. So she knocked on the doors of drugstores all over town, asking for help. Sometimes the doors were closed in her face, but more often than not, people came to her aid.

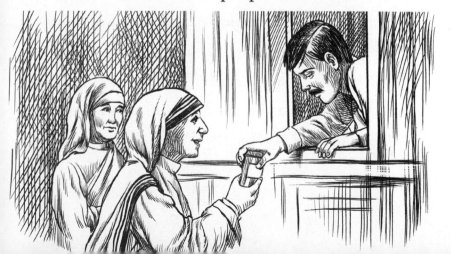

When there was no clean water in Motijhil, Mother Teresa went directly to Dr. B. C. Roy. He was the most important government official in the Bengal region. Dr. Roy had a water pump put in. He later helped with many other things needed in the slums.

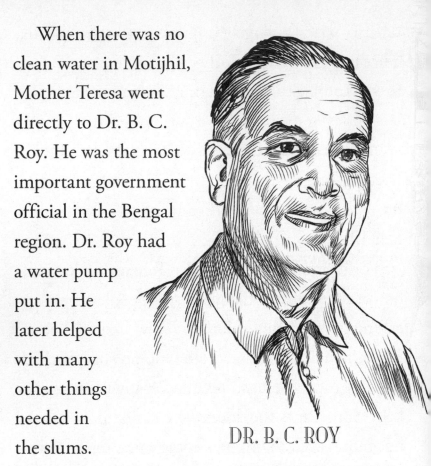

DR. B. C. ROY

Sometimes, help came in surprising ways—big and small. Before Mother Teresa opened Shanti Nagar for lepers, Pope Paul VI came to visit India. He donated the car he used on his Indian trip to the Missionaries of Charity. They raffled it off,

making enough money to start the entire Shanti
Nagar project.

Another story goes that a young boy in India
heard about Mother Teresa. He asked how much
money his family could save if he stopped eating
sugar for a little while. Several days later, the boy
presented Mother Teresa with one rupee—less
than one penny!

Then, in 1969, Malcolm Muggeridge made
a film about Mother Teresa for the British
Broadcasting Company. Muggeridge was a famous
journalist. He was amazed by Mother Teresa's
charity work. When people saw the film on
television, money to the Missionaries of Charity
poured in from all over the world.

In 1972, Mother Teresa received a letter from
Albania. Age was living there with Drana. Age
said their mother was very ill. In Albania, citizens
were not free to travel in and out of the country.

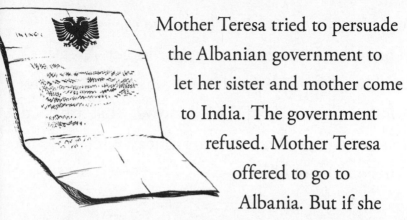 Mother Teresa tried to persuade
the Albanian government to
let her sister and mother come
to India. The government
refused. Mother Teresa
offered to go to
Albania. But if she
did, the government said she might not be able
to return to India. So, "for the sake of the poor,"
Mother Teresa said, she did not go. Her mother
died in July 1972. Her sister, Age, died the very
next summer.

Mother Teresa worked through that sadness.
Word of her charity work in Calcutta spread
over the next ten years. Mother Teresa became
more and more well-known. She received many
awards, including the prestigious Nobel Peace
Prize in 1979. It was for her work "in bringing
help to suffering humanity." Her brother, Lazar,
who lived in Italy until his death in 1981, was

in Oslo, Norway, to see her receive the award. The Nobel Peace Prize brought Mother Teresa worldwide fame. Being famous was never a goal for Mother Teresa. She did see, however, that it helped raise awareness for, and bring money into, the Missionaries of Charity.

Still, with fame came controversy. Some people criticized Mother Teresa for taking money from people who were later convicted of stealing. She had no way of knowing, her defenders said. Some people criticized her for not speaking out against the *causes* of poverty instead of just trying to treat it. Mother Teresa always said she could not change the world. It was the job of politicians to root out poverty.

Others complained about the medical treatment in her facilities. But the Missionaries of Charity was not meant to take the place of trained medical workers. They were there to love the sick and the dying.

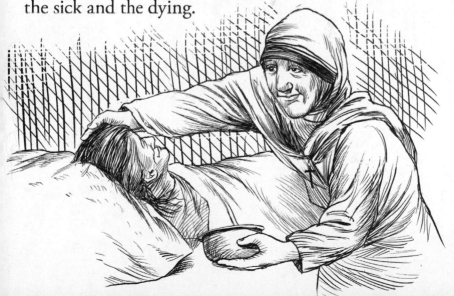

The people they took care of "have been unwanted all their lives," she said. "We want to make them feel, at the end, that someone loves them and someone cares for them."

Still, others argued that Mother Teresa's devotion to the poor was just an excuse to make people become Catholic. But Mother Teresa never tried to convert people to her religion.

Instead, she liked to say, "I convert you to become a better Hindu, a better Catholic, a better Muslim or Buddhist."

Mother Teresa believed that people of all different faiths were praying to the same God. The most important thing was to love one another. "The best conversion is to make the people love one another," she said. "When they love one another, they come closer to God."

THE NOBEL PRIZE

THE NOBEL PEACE PRIZE IS ONE OF THE WORLD'S MOST FAMOUS HONORS. IT IS NAMED AFTER ALFRED NOBEL (1833–1896), A SWEDISH CHEMIST AND INVENTOR. IN HIS WILL, NOBEL ESTABLISHED A FUND UPON HIS DEATH TO AWARD ANNUAL PRIZES IN THE AREAS OF CHEMISTRY, LITERATURE, PEACE, PHYSICS, AND PHYSIOLOGY OR MEDICINE. THE PRIZES WERE FIRST AWARDED IN 1901.

ALFRED NOBEL

THE PEACE PRIZE IS PRESENTED IN OSLO (THE CAPITAL OF NORWAY) EACH YEAR ON DECEMBER 10, THE ANNIVERSARY OF NOBEL'S DEATH.

Chapter 9
Saint Among Us

For almost thirty-five years, Mother Teresa only worked in India. But in 1965, Pope Paul VI gave her permission to open Missionaries of Charity houses around the world. A local bishop in Venezuela invited her to visit, and so she did. Soon after, the Missionaries of Charity house in Cocorote, Venezuela, opened.

The next house outside of India opened in a suburb of Rome, Italy, in 1968. Then came houses in Australia, Africa, England, and elsewhere. In 1971, the Missionaries of Charity opened its first house in the United States, in New York City. In every city, the nuns left the Missionaries of Charity house each morning to go into the streets and help the poor.

In 1982, Mother Teresa led a group into Beirut, Lebanon. This country in the Middle East was in the midst of war. Dozens of children were huddled in a hospital where bombs had blown out windows and torn apart two floors of the building. Mother Teresa, then seventy-two years old, helped pick up children herself and carry them to waiting Red Cross cars. Why did she go into such a dangerous war zone? "They are all the children of God,"

Mother Teresa said. The children were soon taken to safety, to a school the Missionaries of Charity had opened two years earlier.

Becoming a worldwide aid organization was a huge undertaking. But Mother Teresa always shrugged off any questions of how she did it. "We know what people need, and we start doing it," she said matter-of-factly.

How could this tiny, frail-looking nun do so much?

Her old friend Father Van Exem had this explanation: Mother Teresa, he once said, "was an ordinary Loreto nun, a very ordinary person, but with great love for her Lord."

"[She was] always a very pious person, [but] she was just herself," said one nun who worked with Mother Teresa. "She did not force it on anybody. She just was what she felt she had to be."

In the 1980s, Mother Teresa's health began

to fail. Over the years, she had many heart
attacks. She came down with diseases such
as malaria and pneumonia. Against doctors'
advice, though, she pressed on. There were so

many poor to help, she reasoned, and, "I have all eternity to rest." She continued working as the head of the Missionaries of Charity until March 1997.

On September 5, 1997, Mother Teresa died in Calcutta at age eighty-seven.

The Missionaries of Charity continues its work under the leadership of Sister Mary Prema Pierick. It has homes and aid shelters in more than one hundred countries around the world. The charity feeds more than five hundred thousand families, and treats more than ninety thousand leprosy patients each year.

In 2003, Mother Teresa was beatified by the Catholic Church.

Pope John Paul II officially declared her "Blessed Mother Teresa of Calcutta" for a miracle involving the healing of an Indian woman who had cancer. A second miracle, the healing of a Brazilian man, was credited to her by Pope Francis in 2015.

In September 2016, Mother Teresa was canonized—declared a saint—by the Roman Catholic Church.

To many people, saints are impossibly good people who lived hundreds of years ago. But Mother Teresa showed that saints do live among us, even today.

TIMELINE OF
MOTHER TERESA'S LIFE

1910	Born Agnes Gonxha Bojaxhiu on August 27 in Skopje in the Ottoman Empire
1928	Leaves for Ireland and the Loreto Sisters convent
1931	Takes her first vows as a nun. Her new name is Sister Teresa, and she begins teaching at Loreto's St. Mary's School in Calcutta
1937	Takes her final vows as a nun
1944	Becomes the headmistress of St. Mary's School For the rest of her life, she is known as Mother Teresa
	Hears "the call within a call" on a train ride to Darjeeling
	Granted permission by the pope to leave the convent and work with the poor in India
1950	The Missionaries of Charity is officially formed
1952	Nirmal Hriday, the Missionaries of Charity's home for the dying, opens in Calcutta
1955	Also in Calcutta, the Missionaries of Charity opens a home called Shishu Bhavan, for abandoned children
	In Venezuela, the Missionaries of Charity opens its first home outside of India
1979	Awarded the Nobel Peace Prize
1997	Mother Teresa dies at age eighty-seven on September 5
2003	Mother Teresa is beatified by the Catholic Church and is given the title Blessed Teresa of Calcutta
2016	Mother Teresa is made a saint by Pope Francis on September 4

TIMELINE OF THE WORLD

The *Titanic* sinks on its first voyage	1912
World War I begins	1914
World War I ends	1918
A major flu epidemic, which began in 1918, kills between thirty and fifty million people around the world	1919
The stock market crashes in the United States, and the Great Depression begins	1929
World War II begins	1939
World War II ends	1945
India gains independence from Great Britain and is divided into India and Pakistan	1947
Indian leader Mahatma Gandhi is assassinated	1948
John F. Kennedy, the president of the United States, is assassinated	1963
The United States' Neil Armstrong becomes the first person to walk on the moon	1969
Richard Nixon resigns as president of the United States after the Watergate scandal	1974
The Macintosh personal computer is introduced to the world	1984
The Soviet Union collapses	1991
Terrorist attacks of September 11 kill almost three thousand people in the United States	2001

BIBLIOGRAPHY

* Demi. **Mother Teresa**. New York: Margaret K. McElderry Books, 2005.

* Gold, Maya. **Mother Teresa**. New York: DK Publishing, 2008.

* Jacobs, William Jay. **Mother Teresa: Helping the Poor**. Brook Field, CT: The Millbrook Press, 1991.

Rai, Raghu, and Navin Chawla. **Faith and Compassion: The Life and Work of Mother Teresa**. Rockport, MA: Element Books, 1996.

* Ritter, Christie R. **Mother Teresa: Humanitarian & Advocate for the Poor**. Edina, MN: ABDO, 2011.

* Books for young readers

* Ruth, Amy. **Mother Teresa**. Minneapolis, MN: Lerner, 1999.

Slavicek, Louise Chipley. **Mother Teresa: Caring for the World's Poor**. New York: Chelsea House, 2007.

Spink, Kathryn. **Mother Teresa: A Complete Authorized Biography**. New York: HarperCollins, 1997.

Teresa, Mother. **A Simple Path**. Compiled by Lucinda Vardey. New York: Ballantine Books, 1995.

* Tilton, Rafael. **The Importance of Mother Teresa**. San Diego: Lucent Books, 2000.

YOUR HEADQUARTERS FOR HISTORY

Activities, Mad Libs, and sidesplitting jokes!
Discover the Who HQ books beyond the biographies